I0483155

Cover photo: Elizabeth Routh, Corpus Christi Area Office

HAZARD COMMUNICATION

Small Entity Compliance Guide for Employers That Use Hazardous Chemicals

**Occupational Safety and Health Administration
U.S. Department of Labor**

OSHA 3695-03 2014

TABLE OF CONTENTS

I. INTRODUCTION

Chemicals have become an important element of almost every aspect of modern life. All of these chemicals—from cleaning fluids to pharmaceuticals, pesticides, and paints—are produced in workplaces, and may be used in workplaces downstream. While these chemicals have utility and benefits in their applications, they also have the potential to cause adverse effects. These adverse effects include both health hazards (such as carcinogenicity and sensitization), and physical hazards (for example, flammability and reactivity properties). In order to protect workers from these effects—and to reduce the occurrence of chemical source illnesses and injuries—employers need information about the hazards of the chemicals they use, as well as recommended protective measures. Workers have both a right and a need to know this information too, especially so that they can take steps to protect themselves when necessary.

No one knows exactly how many chemicals may be present in American workplaces. The total number of chemical substances that have been developed and registered in the Chemical Abstracts Service Registry reached 60 million in 2011—the last 10 million of those were added in less than two years. Many of them involve innovations such as the application of nanotechnology.

While not all of these chemicals are produced commercially today, this vast number indicates the scope of the potential problems in workplaces with regard to the safe use of chemicals. In addition, most chemical substances are formulated into mixtures for use in the workplace. Therefore, the number of unique chemical mixtures is far greater than the number of substances, and most workers are exposed to mixtures.

According to the Bureau of Labor Statistics (BLS), acute illnesses and injuries due to chemical exposures in the workplace have decreased 42% since the Hazard Communication Standard was first promulgated.

The scope of workplaces in which chemical exposures occur is also very broad. While most people can readily associate working in a chemical manufacturing plant as being a job that involves chemical exposures, there are many other types of facilities where such usage is also commonplace. For example, construction workers may be exposed to paints, lacquers, thinners, asphalt fumes, or crystalline silica. Hair stylists are exposed to chemical dyes and other hair products that contain hazardous chemicals. All of these types of exposures are of concern in terms of protecting workers, and ensuring that chemicals are used safely.

Audience for this Guide

This guide is intended to help small employers comply with the Occupational Safety and Health Administration's (OSHA) Hazard Communication Standard (HCS). The guide is advisory in nature and informational in content. It is not itself a standard or regulation, and it creates no new legal obligations. The employer must refer to the appropriate standard to ensure it is in compliance. In 25 states and two territories, OSHA standards are enforced by the state agency responsible for the OSHA-approved state plan. These states are: Alaska, Arizona, California, Hawaii, Indiana, Iowa, Kentucky, Maryland, Michigan, Minnesota, Nevada, New Mexico, North Carolina, Oregon, Puerto Rico, South Carolina, Tennessee, Utah, Vermont, Virginia, Washington, and Wyoming. Connecticut, Illinois, New Jersey, New York, and the Virgin Islands operate OSHA-approved State Plans that apply only to state and local government employees. State plans must adopt and enforce standards that are either identical to or at least as effective as the Federal OSHA standards.

OSHA's Hazard Communication Standard

OSHA's HCS, 29 CFR 1910.1200, addresses the informational needs of employers and workers with regard to chemicals. The HCS was first promulgated in 1983, and covered the manufacturing sector. It was later expanded to cover all industries where workers are potentially exposed to hazardous chemicals.

In 2012, the HCS was modified to align its provisions with the United Nations' Globally Harmonized System of Classification and Labelling of Chemicals (GHS). Many benefits will result from revising the HCS to be consistent with the GHS. In particular, the GHS helps to ensure that imported chemicals will be accompanied by consistent hazard and precautionary information to protect workers exposed in the U.S. In addition, the revised HCS can facilitate trade in chemicals since it reduces potential barriers posed by differing global requirements for classification and labeling of chemicals.

"Classification" means to identify the relevant data regarding the hazards of a chemical; review those data to ascertain the hazards associated with the chemical; and decide whether the chemical will be classified as hazardous according to the definition of hazardous chemical in this section. In addition, classification for health and physical hazards includes the determination of the degree of hazard, where appropriate, by comparing the data with the criteria for health and physical hazards.

"Label" means an appropriate group of written, printed or graphic information elements concerning a hazardous chemical that is affixed to, printed on, or attached to the immediate container of a hazardous chemical, or to the outside packaging.

"Safety data sheet (SDS)" means written or printed material concerning a hazardous chemical that is prepared in accordance with paragraph (g) of this section.

The HCS is a unique OSHA standard in a number of respects. It incorporates what is referred to as a *downstream flow of information* from chemical manufacturers, importers, and distributors, to employers using the products:

- The standard requires chemical manufacturers and importers to **classify** the hazards of the chemicals they produce or import, and to prepare appropriate **labels** and **safety data sheets** (SDSs) to convey the hazards, as well as recommended protective measures.

- Chemical manufacturers, importers, and distributors must ensure that the containers of these hazardous chemicals are labeled when shipped, and that SDSs are provided downstream with the first shipment and when the SDSs are updated.

Thus, those who know the most about the chemicals—the companies that produce, import, or distribute them—have the responsibility to assess available information, and convey what is needed to downstream employers where the hazardous chemicals are used. The scope of coverage with regard to employers is addressed in paragraph (b)(2) of the standard:

(b)(2) This section applies to any chemical which is known to be present in the workplace in such a manner that employees may be exposed under normal conditions of use or in a foreseeable emergency.

There are a number of definitions that impact the interpretation of this definition of coverage (see box to the left), but most workplaces will be subject to the rule.

As an employer who is a chemical user, you are required to receive labels and SDSs from your suppliers. Employers have responsibilities under the HCS to establish hazard communication programs, and provide workers with access to labels and SDSs, in addition to informing and training these workers. The responsibilities for hazard communication are illustrated in Figure 1.

"Employee" means a worker who may be exposed to hazardous chemicals under normal operating conditions or in foreseeable emergencies. Workers such as office workers or bank tellers who encounter hazardous chemicals only in non-routine, isolated instances are not covered.

"Exposure or exposed" means that an employee is subjected, in the course of employment, to a chemical that is a physical or health hazard, and includes potential (e.g., accidental or possible) exposure. "Subjected" in terms of health hazards includes any route of entry (e.g., inhalation, ingestion, skin contact or absorption.)

"Produce" means to manufacture, process, formulate, blend, extract, generate, emit, or repackage.

"Use" means to package, handle, react, emit, extract, generate as a by-product, or transfer.

This guide addresses employer responsibilities under the HCS. Many of the provisions of the standard apply only to chemical manufacturers, importers, or distributors. This guide will focus on assisting employers that only use but do not produce chemicals, in order to identify the parts of the rule that apply to their facilities, and help them to develop and implement an effective hazard communication program.

The 2012 revisions to the HCS, also referred to as "HazCom 2012" in this document, primarily address how chemical manufacturers and importers classify chemical hazards and prepare required labels and SDSs. If you are not a chemical manufacturer or importer, and you already have a hazard communication program that complies with the original HCS, you will have limited changes to make related to compliance with the revised standard.

Figure 1: How Hazard Communication Works

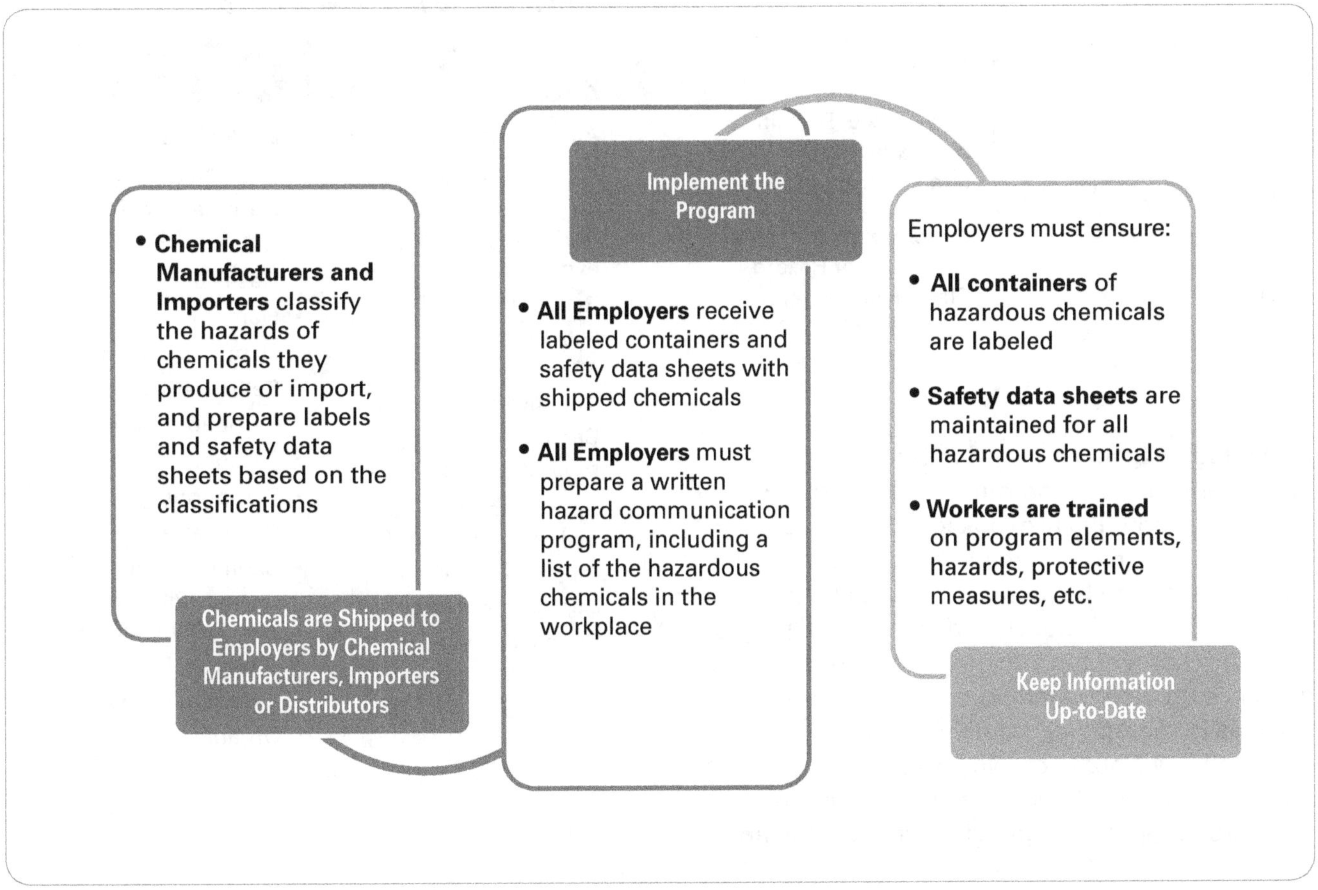

- **Chemical Manufacturers and Importers** classify the hazards of chemicals they produce or import, and prepare labels and safety data sheets based on the classifications

Chemicals are Shipped to Employers by Chemical Manufacturers, Importers or Distributors

Implement the Program

- **All Employers** receive labeled containers and safety data sheets with shipped chemicals

- **All Employers** must prepare a written hazard communication program, including a list of the hazardous chemicals in the workplace

Employers must ensure:

- **All containers** of hazardous chemicals are labeled

- **Safety data sheets** are maintained for all hazardous chemicals

- **Workers are trained** on program elements, hazards, protective measures, etc.

Keep Information Up-to-Date

In order to understand the requirements of HazCom 2012 as applied to your workplace, it is useful to have a general familiarity with the organization of the standard. It is divided into regulatory paragraphs that describe requirements, which are further supplemented by appendices that contain specific details.

Organization of the Regulatory Requirements for Hazard Communication

Paragraphs of the Standard	Appendices to the Standard
(a) Purpose	Appendix A, Health Hazard Criteria (Mandatory)
(b) Scope and Application	
	Appendix B, Physical Hazard Criteria (Mandatory)
(c) Definitions	
(d) Hazard Classification	
	Appendix C, Allocation of Label Elements (Mandatory)
(e) Written Hazard Communication Program	
(f) Labels and Other Forms of Warning	Appendix D, Safety Data Sheets (Mandatory)
(g) Safety Data Sheets	Appendix E, Definition of "Trade Secret" (Mandatory)
(h) Employee Information and Training	
(i) Trade Secrets	Appendix F, Guidance for Hazard Classifications re: Carcinogenicity (Non-Mandatory)
(j) Effective Dates	

Under the HCS, an employer must prepare and implement a hazard communication program for workers potentially exposed to hazardous chemicals. The requirements most relevant to this responsibility can be found in paragraphs (e), (f), (g), and (h) as listed above and indicated in purple. The other parts of the standard may provide some guidance on understanding the requirements (such as Paragraph (c) Definitions), but your responsibilities are to employees in your workplace, and those responsibilities are specified in the standard paragraphs highlighted in the table above.

As previously mentioned, your suppliers must provide hazard information in the form of labels on containers and SDSs when you receive a chemical. The focus of the information is to provide the identities and hazards of the chemicals, their characteristics and properties, and how potential adverse effects can be prevented. A *"hazardous chemical"* means any chemical which is classified as a physical hazard or a health hazard, a simple asphyxiant, combustible dust, pyrophoric gas, or hazard not otherwise classified.

In addition to the health and physical hazards listed above, there may be some hazards that do not meet the specified criteria for the physical and health hazard classes provided in HazCom 2012. In these cases, the chemical manufacturer or importer will designate the hazards as "hazards not otherwise classified" (HNOC), and must provide information on the SDS to ensure that downstream employers are aware of these other effects and any appropriate protective measures.

HCS Health and Physical Hazards

Health Hazards	Physical Hazards
• Acute toxicity	• Explosives
• Skin corrosion/ irritation	• Flammable gases
• Serious eye damage/ eye irritation	• Flammable aerosols
• Respiratory or skin sensitization	• Oxidizing gases
• Germ cell mutagenicity	• Gases under pressure
• Carcinogenicity	• Flammable liquids
• Reproductive toxicity	• Flammable solids
• Specific target organ toxicity – single and repeated exposure	• Self-reactive chemicals
• Aspiration hazard	• Pyrophoric liquids
• Simple asphyxiant	• Pyrophoric solids
	• Pyrophoric gas
	• Self-heating chemicals
	• Chemicals which in contact with water, emit flammable gases
	• Oxidizing liquids
	• Oxidizing solids
	• Organic peroxides
	• Corrosive to metals
	• Combustible dust

HazCom 2012 refers to each of the defined hazards as a *"hazard class."* Most of these hazard classes are subsequently divided into one or more *"hazard category(ies)."* This classification is done by the chemical manufacturer or importer, and is based on the severity of the effect, and the type of data available to indicate each effect. This is important to employers because it leads directly to the information that is subsequently provided on labels and SDSs for the chemical. For example, there are four categories in the hazard class for flammable liquids. These categories are based primarily on flashpoints, so the lower the flashpoint, the more severe the effect. The warnings provided on labels will reflect this severity in different statements depending on which category the chemical falls into based on its flashpoint. The category itself does not appear on the label, but it is available on the SDS for the employer's reference. As an example of hazard categories under HazCom 2012, the following is the criteria for categorizing chemicals classified as flammable liquids:

Criteria for Flammable Liquids

Category	Criteria
1	Flash point < 23°C (73.4°F) and initial boiling point ≤ 35°C (95°F)
2	Flash point < 23°C (73.4°F) and initial boiling point > 35°C (95°F)
3	Flash point ≥ 23°C (73.4°F) and ≤ 60°C (140°F)
4	Flash point > 60°C (140°F) and ≤ 93°C (199.4°F)

As an employer who uses but does not manufacture or import chemicals, you are not responsible for making classifications or evaluating the hazards of a chemical. You must receive a label and SDS from your supplier based on the classification the supplier has made given the available scientific data on the product. All of the criteria used by the chemical manufacturer or importer to perform the classification are provided in HazCom 2012 in Appendices A and B.

Employers are allowed to perform their own classifications if they choose not to rely on the information provided by the chemical manufacturer or importer. If you choose to perform your own classification you will need to comply with the requirements in Appendices A and B of the standard.

If you choose to rely on the classification performed by the manufacturer or importer, it is not necessary to be familiar with the criteria for classifying the chemicals, or the scientific data supporting classification. However, you must have a basic understanding of the hazardous effects caused by the chemicals in your workplace. You must also have such an understanding in order to use the information to select protective measures, and ensure proper management of the chemicals in your workplace. Additionally, you must include information on the different types of hazards of the chemicals used in your workplace and how workers can protect themselves in your information and training program.

Compliance Dates

The first compliance date of importance is *December 1, 2013*. By that date, you must train your employees about the format and presentation of the new labels and SDSs they will be seeing in the workplace. Over the course of several years, your suppliers will be updating labels and SDSs to comply with the new requirements. It is, therefore, important to ensure that you and your employees are able to access and use the information provided in the new approach. All new labels and SDSs must be finished by *June 1, 2015*; however, if you order from a distributer you may still receive labels compliant with HazCom 1994 (the hazard communication standard issued in 1994 and replaced in 2012 by the revised standard) until *December 1, 2015*. If an employer identifies new hazards after December 1, 2015 due to the reclassification of the hazardous chemicals, it has six months, until *June 1, 2016*, to ensure that those hazards are included in the hazard communication program, workplace labeling reflects those new hazards, and employees are trained on the new hazards. During the transition from current requirements to the new requirements, employers may comply with either HazCom 1994 or HazCom 2012, both of which require a hazard communication program.

HazCom 2012 – Complete Schedule of Effective Dates

Effective Completion Date	Requirement(s)	Who
December 1, 2013	Train employees on the new label elements and SDS format.	Employers
June 1, 2015 **December 1, 2015**	Comply with all modified provisions of HazCom 2012, except: Distributors may ship products labeled by the manufacturer or importer under the old system until December 1, 2015.	Chemical manufacturers, importers, distributors and employers
June 1, 2016	Update alternative workplace labeling and hazard communication program as necessary, and provide additional employee training for newly-identified physical or health hazards.	Employers
Transition Period	Comply with either HazCom 2012, HazCom 1994, or both.	All chemical manufacturers, importers, distributors and employers

II. STEPS TO AN EFFECTIVE HAZARD COMMUNICATION PROGRAM

All workplaces where workers are exposed to hazardous chemicals must have a written hazard communication program that describes how the HazCom standard is implemented in that facility. When hazard communication is implemented effectively, it has significant benefits for both the employer and the workers in a workplace. Employers need the information provided to them in order to assess the safety and health aspects of their workplace appropriately, and to select needed control measures for the chemicals that are present. The information provided on SDSs may also be used by employers to select the least hazardous chemical available to accomplish what is needed in the workplace. Substitution of a less hazardous chemical benefits workers because they will not be exposed to the greater hazards, and benefits employers because they may have less need for controls in some situations. The information employers receive on labels and SDSs will help them meet requirements for a safe and healthful workplace.

> An effective hazard communication program benefits both workers and employers. The information provided by suppliers allows employers to design and implement a chemical safety and health management program.

Workers are entitled to the information about the identities and hazards of the chemicals they are potentially exposed to when working. When workers have such information, they are able to take steps to protect themselves, and to implement the controls their employer has selected for them. Knowing the health effects is important so that any signs or symptoms of exposure can be evaluated. Furthermore, being aware of the chemicals and associated hazards can help the worker determine how the exposure may affect preexisting medical conditions.

> In a survey conducted by the U.S. Government Accountability Office (GAO), approximately 30% of responding small businesses indicated they used information on SDSs to find less hazardous chemicals to use in their workplaces.

Some employers view hazard communication as merely a "paper exercise," regarding compliance as just making sure that all the required labels and SDSs are available, but not using the information. Hazard communication is much more than a paper exercise when implemented properly. The proper use of the information by employers to control chemical exposure results in a decrease in illnesses and injuries caused by chemicals in the workplace—a clear benefit for exposed workers. Effective hazard communication also helps with effective management of chemicals in the workplace, resulting in increased productivity, decreased workers' compensation costs, and other employer benefits.

The HCS includes a three-part approach to communicating information to downstream employers, as well as workers.

- Labeling containers of hazardous chemicals, which serves as an immediate warning of hazards
- SDSs, which are sources of detailed information on the hazardous chemical
- Training on the hazards

An effective hazard communication program can be accomplished in six steps (Figure 2).

Figure 2: Six Steps to an Effective Hazard Communication Program

1. Learn the Standard/Identify Responsible Staff	• Obtain a copy of OSHA's Hazard Communication Standard. • Become familiar with its provisions. • Make sure that someone has primary responsibility for coordinating implementation. • Identify staff for particular activities (e.g., training).
2. Prepare and Implement a Written Hazard Communication Program	• Prepare a written plan to indicate how hazard communication will be addressed in your facility. • Prepare a list or inventory of all hazardous chemicals in the workplace.
3. Ensure Containers are Labeled	• Keep labels on shipped containers. • Label workplace containers where required.
4. Maintain Safety Data Sheets	• Maintain safety data sheets for each hazardous chemical in the workplace. • Ensure that safety data sheets are readily accessible to employees.
5. Inform and Train Employees	• Train employees on the hazardous chemicals in their work area before initial assignment, and when new hazards are introduced. • Include the requirements of the standard, hazards of chemicals, appropriate protective measures, and where and how to obtain additional information.
6. Evaluate and Reassess Your Program	• Review your hazard communication program periodically to make sure that it is still working and meeting its objectives. • Revise your program as appropriate to address changed conditions in the workplace (e.g., new chemicals, new hazards, etc.).

<table>
<tr><td>

1. Learn the Standard/Identify Responsible Staff

</td><td>

- Obtain a copy of OSHA's Hazard Communication Standard.
- Become familiar with its provisions.
- Make sure that someone has primary responsibility for coordinating implementation.
- Identify staff for particular activities (e.g., training).

</td></tr>
</table>

You are already on your way to accomplishing Step 1 by reading this guide. It is always best to review the actual provisions of the standard to ensure you are in full compliance. OSHA provides online access to the standard, as well as guidance, interpretations, and other relevant materials on its hazard communication web page: www.osha.gov/dsg/hazcom. The full regulatory text can be found at: www.osha.gov/dsg/hazcom/HCSFinalRegTxt.html.

As noted above, the provisions that apply to employers simply using chemicals in the workplace, rather than those that produce or import chemicals, are found primarily in the following paragraphs:

> *(e) Written Hazard Communication Program;*
> *(f) Labels and Other Forms of Warning;*
> *(g) Safety Data Sheets; and*
> *(h) Employee Information and Training.*

You can focus on the requirements in these paragraphs to determine what is needed for compliance in your workplace. There may also be other provisions of the standard that help establish compliance requirements in some workplaces.

Paragraph (b), Scope and Application, specifies two types of work operations where the coverage of the rule is limited. These are laboratories and operations where chemicals are only handled in sealed containers (e.g., a warehouse). Employers with these types of work operations have reduced obligations under the HCS and basically only need to keep labels on containers as they are received; maintain SDSs that are received, and give employees access to them; and provide information and training to employees.

Laboratories and operations where chemicals are only handled in sealed containers do not have to have written hazard communication programs and lists of chemicals.

The limited coverage for laboratories and sealed container operations addresses your obligation to your own workers in the operations involved. However, when laboratory employers or employers where only sealed containers are involved act as chemical manufacturers, distributors or importers, they must fulfill their duties as suppliers. For example, in warehouse operations where the employees are only exposed to sealed containers, paragraph (b)(4) of the standard would apply. When these chemicals are distributed to downstream users, paragraph (b)(4) requires the company to provide HazCom 2012-compliant labels and SDSs to downstream customers at the time of the first shipment and when the SDS is updated.

Paragraph (c), Definitions, can be used to determine the meaning of some provisions in HazCom 2012 through the definitions provided for the terms used in them. This guide will highlight some of these definitions, but you may want to consult the definitions for other terms to help ensure you fully understand your compliance obligations in the workplace.

Hazard communication must be a continuing program in your facility. Compliance with the HCS is not a "one shot deal." In order to have a successful program, it will be necessary to assign responsibility to staff for both the initial and ongoing activities needed to comply with the standard. In some cases, these activities may already be part of current job assignments. For example, site supervisors are frequently responsible for on-the-job training sessions. Early identification of the responsible workers, and their involvement in the development of your plan of action, will result in a more effective program design.

In order to ensure you have an effective program and address all of the necessary components, responsibility for implementation of hazard communication should be assigned to someone to coordinate. While different people may be responsible for certain parts of implementation, there should nevertheless be someone who has overall responsibility. Approaching compliance consistently, and comprehensively, is the key to success.

The person responsible for the overall coordination may not be the best person to accomplish all of the elements. For example, training workers may require different expertise than coordinating compliance. The standard allows employers the flexibility to do what is best in their own facilities as long as compliance with all elements is achieved.

2. Prepare and Implement a Written Hazard Communication Program

- Prepare a written plan to indicate how hazard communication will be addressed in your facility.
- Prepare a list or inventory of all hazardous chemicals in the workplace.

Paragraph (e), Written Hazard Communication Program, requires employers to prepare and implement a written hazard communication program. This does not need to be lengthy or complicated. The main intent of the requirement is to help ensure that compliance with the standard is done in a systematic way and that all elements are coordinated. Thus, the program must describe how the employer will address the requirements of paragraphs (f) Labels and Other Forms of Warning; (g) Safety Data Sheets; and (h) Employee Information and Training, in the workplace. A sample written program is provided in Appendix A of this guide.

In addition, the written program must include the following items:

■ *Paragraph (e)(1): A list of the hazardous chemicals known to be present in the workplace.* The list may be kept using any *product identifier* from the SDS. Thus, the list may be kept by product name, common name, or chemical name. The important aspect of this requirement is that the term used on the list must also be available on both the SDS and the label so that these documents can be cross-referenced. The list can be compiled in whatever way the employer finds most useful and applicable to the workplace. A list of all hazardous chemicals in the entire workplace may be most suitable for very small facilities, where there are few work areas and all workers are potentially exposed to essentially the same products. For larger workplaces, it may be more convenient to compile lists of hazardous chemicals by work area and have them assembled together as the overall list for the workplace.

The list is an inventory of chemicals for which the employer must ensure that there is an SDS available. Compiling the list also helps employers keep track of the chemicals present, and to identify chemicals that are no longer being used, and thus could be removed from the workplace. Removing such chemicals may also reduce potential adverse effects that could occur in the workplace.

The best way to prepare a comprehensive list may be to survey the workplace. Purchasing records may also help and employers should establish procedures to ensure that purchasing procedures result in receiving SDSs before a material is used in the workplace. Prior to purchasing chemicals, review the hazards of the chemicals and evaluate if less hazardous chemicals can be used instead.

> "Product identifier" means the name or number used for a hazardous chemical on a label or in the SDS. It provides a unique means by which the user can identify the chemical. The product identifier used shall permit cross-references to be made among the list of hazardous chemicals required in the written hazard communication program, the label and the SDS.

The broadest possible perspective should be taken when doing the survey. Sometimes people think of "chemicals" as being only liquids in containers. The HCS covers chemicals in all forms—liquids, solids, gases, vapors, fumes, and mists—whether they are "contained" or not. The hazardous nature of the chemical and the potential for exposure are the factors that determine whether a chemical is covered. If the chemical is not hazardous, it is not covered by the standard. If there is no potential for exposure (e.g., the chemical is inextricably bound and cannot be released), the chemical is not covered by the standard.

Look around. Identify chemicals in containers, including pipes, but also think about chemicals that are generated during work operations. For example, welding fumes, dusts, and exhaust fumes are all sources of chemical exposures. Read the labels provided by suppliers for hazard information. Make a list of all chemicals in the workplace that are potentially hazardous. For your own information and planning, you may also want to note on the list the location(s) of the products within the workplace, and an indication of the hazards as found on the label. This will help as you prepare the rest of your program.

Paragraph (b) of the standard, scope and application, includes exemptions for various chemicals or workplace situations. After compiling the complete list of chemicals, you should review paragraph (b) to determine if any of the items can be eliminated from the list because they are exempted materials. For example, food, drugs, and cosmetics brought into the workplace for personal consumption by workers are exempt.

Once you have compiled a complete list of the potentially hazardous chemicals in the workplace, the next step is to determine if you have received SDSs for all of them. Check your files against the inventory you have just compiled. Employers are required to have SDSs for all hazardous chemicals that they use. If any are missing, contact your supplier and request one. It is a good idea to document these requests, either by keeping a copy of a letter or e-mail, or a note regarding telephone conversations. If you cannot show a good faith effort to receive the SDS, you can be cited for not having the SDS for a hazardous chemical. If you have SDSs for chemicals that are not on your list, figure out why. Maybe you do not use the chemical anymore. Or maybe you missed

it in your survey. Some suppliers provide SDSs for products that are not hazardous. These SDSs do not have to be maintained.

Do not allow workers to use any hazardous chemicals for which you have not received an SDS. The SDS provides information you need to ensure that proper protective measures are implemented prior to worker exposure.

■ *Paragraph (e)(1)(ii): Methods to inform employees of the hazards of non-routine tasks.* The written program needs to include how an employer will inform workers of hazards that are outside of their normal work routine. While workers' initial training will address the types of exposures they will encounter in their usual work routines, there may be other tasks to be performed on occasion that will expose these workers to different hazards, as well as require novel control measures. For example, in a manufacturing facility, it may be necessary periodically to drain and clean out reactor vessels. For this task, workers may be exposed to cleaning chemicals that are not normally in the workplace, and the usual controls for the process may not protect them, so personal protective equipment may have to be worn. The written program needs to address how the employer will handle such situations and make sure that workers involved have the necessary information to stay protected.

■ *Paragraph (e)(2): Multi-Employer Workplaces.* Where there is more than one employer operating on a site, and employees may be exposed to the chemicals used by each employer, the employer's written hazard communication program must address:

— How on-site access to SDSs will be provided to the other employer(s).

— How such employers will be informed of needed precautionary measures.

— How such employers will be informed of the on-site labeling system if it is different from the labels specified for shipped containers under the standard.

In summary, if you are not a new employer, you should already have a written hazard communication program for your workplace. Review your written program to ensure that it is consistent with the HazCom 2012 requirements. It may need to be updated; for example, you may have to add or delete chemicals from the list in the program, or change your description of the approach to workplace labeling.

If your workers' job assignment requires travel between various geographical locations, you may keep the written program at the primary work location.

Many trade associations and other professional groups have provided sample programs and other assistance materials to employers. These have been very helpful to many employers since they tend to be tailored to the particular industry involved. You may wish to investigate whether your industry trade groups have developed such materials. Additionally, a sample written hazard communication program is included in Appendix A to this guide.

Although such general guidance may be helpful, you must remember that the written program has to reflect what you are doing in your workplace. Therefore, if you use a generic program it must be adapted to address the facility that it actually covers. For example, the written plan must list the chemicals present at the site, indicate who is to be responsible for the various aspects of the program in your facility, and indicate where written materials will be made available to workers.

If OSHA inspects your workplace, the OSHA Compliance Safety and Health Officer (CSHO) will ask to see your written plan.

3. Ensure Containers are Labeled

• Keep labels on shipped containers.
• Label workplace containers where required.

Labels are the first part **(paragraph (f) Labels and Other Forms of Warning)** of the three-part approach to communicating information downstream mentioned earlier. A label must be on the immediate container of every hazardous chemical. The label is an immediate type of warning since it is present in the work area, right on the actual container of a hazardous chemical. It is a snapshot of the hazards and protective information related to the chemical, and a summary of the more detailed information available on the SDS.

When you purchase a hazardous chemical from a supplier, you will receive a container that is labeled with the information required under the HCS. Employers can rely on the information provided by their suppliers. The label requirements in the HCS changed significantly with the publication of HazCom 2012. Under the prior standard, chemical manufacturers and importers were required to convey the hazards and identity of the products, but were not given specifications on how this was to be done. As a result, labels varied in terms of how the information was conveyed, the terminology used, and the design of the label. This made it more difficult for employers and workers to access and comprehend the information presented than if chemical manufacturers and importers follow the same approach.

The label requirements for the revised standard are more specific, which will lead to increased uniformity. This should benefit employers and workers by providing the information in standardized language and graphics, making it easier to understand, and helping to ensure that labels on containers of the same chemical from different suppliers have the same information.

HazCom 2012 provides chemical manufacturers and importers the information to be conveyed once they have determined the hazard of a chemical. The labels you receive on a shipped container must have the following information, located together (other information may also appear on the label):

- Product identifier
- Signal word
- Hazard statement(s)
- Pictogram(s)
- Precautionary statement(s)
- Name, address, and phone number of the responsible party

- The **product identifier** is any chemical, common, or trade name or designation that the chemical manufacturer or importer chooses to use on the label. The term must also appear on the SDS. The signal word, hazard statement(s), pictogram(s), and precautionary statement(s) are the **label elements** that comprise the primary information about hazards and protective measures on the label.

- A **signal word** is a word used to indicate the relative level of severity of hazard and alert the reader to a potential hazard on the label. The signal words used in the standard are *"danger"* and *"warning."* "Danger" is used for the more severe hazards, while "warning" is used for the less severe hazards. Signal words were not previously used in the HCS, although they do often appear on consumer labels. It is important to be aware of—and train workers on—the way signal words convey a difference in the severity of the hazard. While the product is hazardous wherever a signal word is indicated, the signal word chosen can give a preliminary idea of the relative significance of the effect.

- A **hazard statement** is a statement assigned to a hazard class and category that describes the nature of the hazard(s) of a chemical, including, where appropriate, the degree of hazard. **Example: Fatal if swallowed.**

- The hazard statement(s) for a hazardous chemical describe the hazard(s) in text, in a simple, direct manner. There is a hazard statement for each hazard category of a hazard class, and it will vary depending on the degree of hazard. The example presented above is a hazard statement for acute oral toxicity. The hazard statement conveys that the chemical is severely toxic, and ingestion of the chemical results in death. But for less toxic chemicals, the hazard statement may be "toxic if swallowed" or "harmful if swallowed." As with the signal words, this information conveys the relative severity of the hazard, which impacts how it is handled and controlled.

- A **pictogram** is a composition that may include a symbol plus other graphic elements, such as a border, background pattern, or color, that is intended to convey specific information about the hazards of a chemical. Eight pictograms are designated under this standard for application to a hazard category. Under HazCom 2012, pictograms are black symbols, on a white background, with a red diamond border. For example, this is the pictogram for oxidizers:

Pictograms are an important addition to the hazard communication tools in the standard. A pictogram draws the attention of a label reader, and you and your workers should be aware that the appearance of a pictogram in a red diamond frame means that a hazard of concern is present in the product. Some of the pictograms in the standard have symbols that resemble the hazardous effect, and others are merely meant to attract attention. Pictograms may be used for several different hazardous effects as well (see Figure 3).

Pictograms have long been used internationally because they convey information without text. This allows users who are either literate in a different language than that used on the label or who are not literate at all to understand that the chemical is hazardous.

One of the systems that has long used pictograms is the international transport system. This system has been adopted by the U.S. Department of Transportation (DOT), and is familiar to those who handle shipping containers in the United States. The symbols have been harmonized as much as possible for the hazards covered both in transport and in the workplace. While both pictograms are diamond-shaped, the transport system's pictograms have backgrounds of various colors. Where the shipping container is also the container used in the workplace, workers must be made aware of the DOT pictograms[1], as they may appear on the label in addition to, or instead of, the HazCom 2012 pictograms used to represent the same hazard. See Figure 4 for examples of DOT pictograms. Note that the environment pictogram located in the center of the bottom row in Figure 3 is not required under the OSHA standard since OSHA does not regulate environmental hazards. However, you may see this pictogram used on labels and SDSs to convey environmental hazards, and that will provide useful information for you to use in managing your chemicals.

---

1. The U.S. Department of Transportation (DOT) uses the terms transport "placards" or "labels" to refer to the diamond-shaped (square on point) graphic elements that are used to identify shipments of hazardous materials. However, for the purpose of this document, these graphic elements are referred to as "pictograms." More information on DOT placards or labels may be found at www.dot.gov.

Figure 3: HazCom 2012 Pictograms

Health Hazard	Flame	Exclamation Mark
• Carcinogen • Mutagenicity • Reproductive Toxicity • Respiratory Sensitizer • Target Organ Toxicity • Aspiration Toxicity	• Flammables • Pyrophorics • Self-Heating • Emits Flammable Gas • Self-Reactives • Organic Peroxides	• Irritant (skin and eye) • Skin Sensitizer • Acute Toxicity (harmful) • Narcotic Effects • Respiratory Tract Irritant • Hazardous to Ozone Layer (Non-Mandatory)
Gas Cylinder	**Corrosion**	**Exploding Bomb**
• Gases Under Pressure	• Skin Corrosion/ Burns • Eye Damage • Corrosive to Metals	• Explosives • Self-Reactives • Organic Peroxides
Flame Over Circle	**Environment** (Non-Mandatory)	**Skull and Crossbones**
• Oxidizers	• Aquatic Toxicity	• Acute Toxicity (fatal or toxic)

Figure 4: Examples of Transport Pictograms

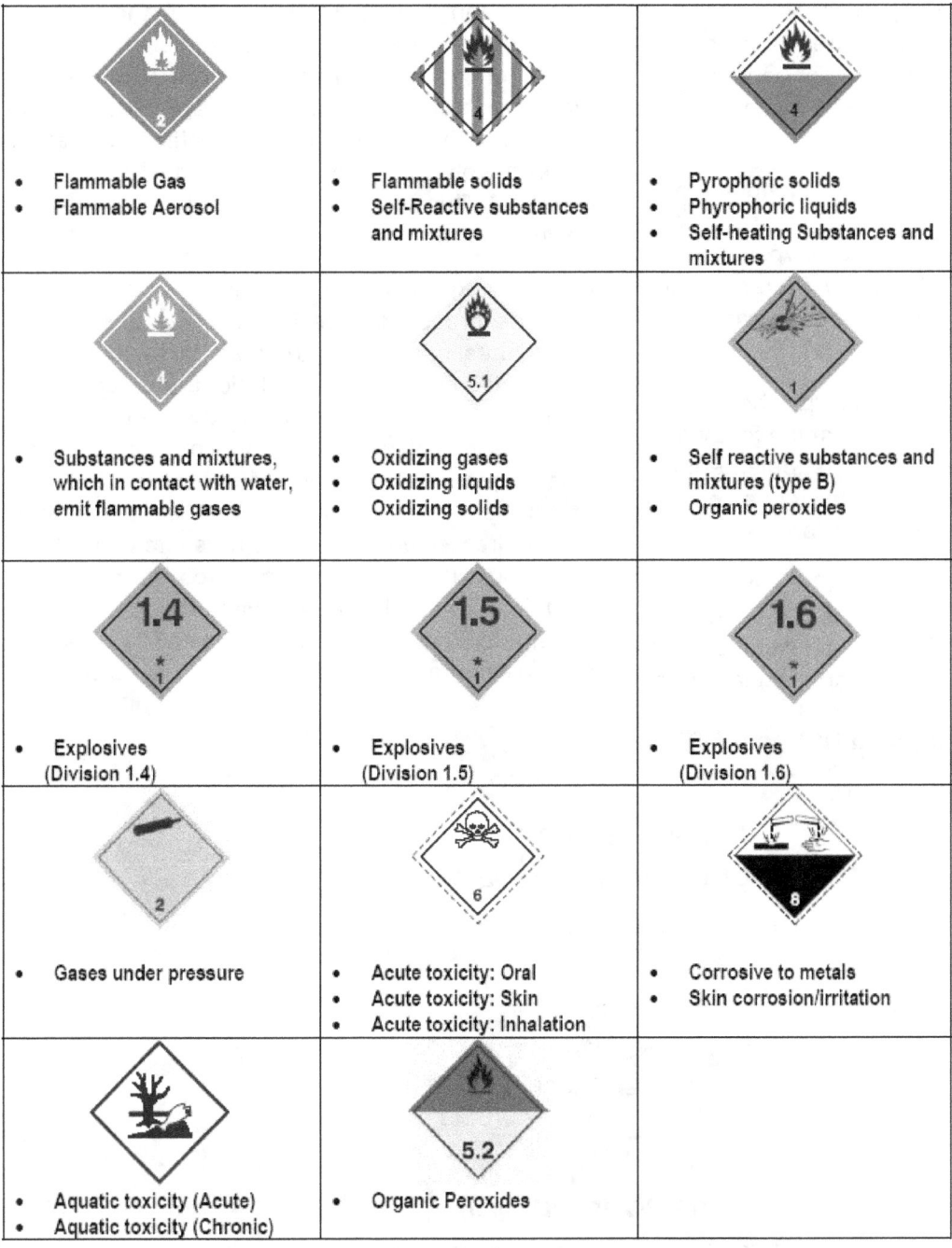

• Flammable Gas • Flammable Aerosol	• Flammable solids • Self-Reactive substances and mixtures	• Pyrophoric solids • Phyrophoric liquids • Self-heating Substances and mixtures
• Substances and mixtures, which in contact with water, emit flammable gases	• Oxidizing gases • Oxidizing liquids • Oxidizing solids	• Self reactive substances and mixtures (type B) • Organic peroxides
• Explosives (Division 1.4)	• Explosives (Division 1.5)	• Explosives (Division 1.6)
• Gases under pressure	• Acute toxicity: Oral • Acute toxicity: Skin • Acute toxicity: Inhalation	• Corrosive to metals • Skin corrosion/irritation
• Aquatic toxicity (Acute) • Aquatic toxicity (Chronic)	• Organic Peroxides	

■ A *precautionary statement* is a phrase that describes recommended measures that should be taken to minimize or prevent adverse effects resulting from exposure to a hazardous chemical, or improper storage or handling. **Example: Do not eat, drink, or smoke when using this product.**

Precautionary statements are key to helping you decide what you need to do to protect workers and your workplace. There are four types of statements: *Prevention, Response, Storage, and Disposal.* These have been assigned to hazard classes and categories.

Therefore, a compliant HazCom 2012 label on a shipped container will have at least the following information as shown in Figure 5 (supplemental information is permitted as long as it does not conflict with the required information).

You are required by paragraph (f)(6) of the standard to ensure that containers of hazardous chemicals in your workplace are labeled. For those containers that are received already labeled from the supplier, and are used in the workplace, simply maintaining the label received from the supplier is the best and easiest option. However, the standard is flexible, and employers may relabel these containers, or label other containers used in the workplace with various options as long as workers have immediate access to the specific information about the physical and health hazards of the chemical. This could be included in the workplace hazard communication program.

Under paragraph (f)(7), employers may use signs, placards, process sheets, batch tickets, operating procedures, or other written material instead of affixing labels to individual stationary process containers, as long as the alternative method identifies which containers it applies to and conveys at least general information regarding the hazards of the chemicals. Paragraph (f)(8) of the standard also addresses portable containers into which the hazardous chemicals are transferred from a labeled container, and which are for the immediate use of the employee who performs the transfer. These portable containers do not have to be labeled.

Figure 5: Example of Required HCS Label Elements

Product Identifier
Pictogram *(Symbol in Red Frame)*

Signal Word *(Danger)*
Hazard Statement(s) *(Extremely flammable gas)*

Precautionary Statement(s) *(Keep away from heat and open flames. No smoking.*
Leaking gas fire: Do not extinguish, unless leak can be stopped safely. Eliminate all ignition
sources if safe to do so. Store in well-ventilated place.)

Name, Address, and Telephone Number
of Manufacturer, Importer, or Other Responsible Party

Some employers use third-party workplace label systems, such as those that have numerical ratings to indicate the hazards (e.g., National Fire Protection Association (NFPA) or Hazardous Materials Identification System (HMIS)). These may be used in conjunction with the supplemental information on the label to ensure that workers have complete information, as long as the ratings are consistent with the hazard definitions in HazCom 2012, i.e., the criteria used to assign the numerical ratings reflects the hazard categories in each hazard class in HazCom 2012. One note with regard to numerical ratings—these systems generally use the number 1 to indicate the lowest degree of hazard, and the number 4 as the highest degree. This is the opposite of the hazard category numbering in HazCom 2012. Therefore, if as an employer you are preparing such labels based on information on the SDS, you must ensure that the numbers are properly applied to reflect the accurate degree of hazard information. Category numbers do not appear on HazCom 2012 shipped container labels, and are not equivalent to the hazard rating systems.

> HazCom 2012 hazard category numbers are not required to appear on shipped container labels, and are not equivalent to the NFPA and HMIS hazard rating systems.

The employer must make sure that labels in the workplace are legible and prominently displayed. While the label information must be in English, employers are free to add warnings in other languages if workers would find that helpful. OSHA has prepared QuickCards™ to describe the label elements (OSHA 3492), as well as illustrate the pictograms (OSHA 3491). These are available on the OSHA web page, or can be obtained from your local OSHA area office.

If your workplace is inspected by OSHA, CSHOs will be looking for at least the following aspects of your labeling approach:

1. Designation of person(s) responsible for ensuring compliant labeling of shipped and in-plant containers;

2. Description of written alternatives to labeling of stationary process containers (if used);

3. Appropriate labels on all workplace containers, including those received from a supplier, secondary containers, and stationary process containers;

4. A description and explanation of labels on both shipped and workplace containers included in the employee training program; and,

5. Procedures to review and update workplace label information when necessary.

4. Maintain Safety Data Sheets

- Maintain safety data sheets for each hazardous chemical in the workplace.
- Ensure that safety data sheets are readily accessible to employees.

The second part in the approach to communicating information in HazCom 2012 is to maintain SDSs (**paragraph (g) Safety Data Sheets and Mandatory Appendix D**). The SDSs are the source of detailed information on hazardous chemicals. This includes information for many different audiences—employers, workers, safety and health professionals, emergency responders, government agencies, and consumers. It is difficult for one document to serve the needs of all of these different audiences since some require much more technical information than others. Therefore, the SDS sections have generally been organized so that the information of most use to exposed workers, emergency responders, and others who do not need extensive technical detail is in the beginning of the SDS, while the more technical information most commonly read by health and safety professionals is located in the later sections. For example, a description of a chemical's health effects appears in Section 2, hazard identification, but the toxicological data upon which the determination of these effects is based appears in Section 11, toxicological information. All of the sections are available to any reader, but there is a difference between what is necessary for a broader audience (workers and emergency responders, for example), and what might be needed by others designing protective measures or providing medical services.

The SDS requirements in HazCom 2012 are based on an internationally agreed upon 16-section SDS. This format is based on ANSI Z400.1[2], so it

is most likely already familiar to your employees. HazCom 2012 establishes section headings for the SDS, as well as the order in which they are to be provided, and the minimum information required to be included in each section under Appendix D of the standard. However, the information in some of the sections are non-mandatory because they address information that involve the requirements of other government bodies, and thus are not under OSHA's jurisdiction. Even though these sections are not considered mandatory by OSHA, the headings are still required to be present on the SDS. They will provide useful information for you to address other requirements you may need to follow. The sixteen sections are as follows, with the non-mandatory sections indicated in italics:

1. Identification
2. Hazard(s) identification
3. Composition/information on ingredients
4. First-aid measures
5. Firefighting measures
6. Accidental release measures
7. Handling and storage
8. Exposure control/personal protection
9. Physical and chemical properties
10. Stability and reactivity
11. Toxicological information
12. *Ecological information*
13. *Disposal considerations*
14. *Transport information*
15. *Regulatory information*
16. Other information

Chemical manufacturers and importers are required to obtain or develop an SDS for each hazardous chemical they produce or import. Chemical manufacturers, importers, and

[2] The first American National Standard Institute (ANSI) standard developed to assist in the preparation of safety data sheets (*American National Standard for Hazardous Industrial Chemicals–Material Safety Data Sheets–Preparation)* was issued in 1993. This standard was updated in 1998 and 2004. In 2010, it was combined with ANSI Z129 and renamed, *American National Standard for Hazardous Workplace Chemicals–Hazard Evaluation and Safety Data Sheet and Precautionary Labeling Preparation.*

distributors are responsible for ensuring that their customers are provided a copy of these SDSs, at the time of the first shipment, and when an SDS is updated with new and significant information. Employers must have an SDS for each hazardous chemical which they use. Employers may rely on the information received from their suppliers unless they know the information is incorrect. If you do not receive an SDS automatically, you must request one as soon as possible. If you receive an SDS that is obviously inadequate, with, for example, blank spaces, you must request an appropriately completed one. If your request for an SDS or for a corrected SDS does not produce the information needed, you should contact your local OSHA area office for assistance in obtaining the SDS. Employers must maintain the current version of the SDS; if a new SDS is received with a shipment, they must maintain and make available the new SDS.

The SDSs must be in English. Many larger manufacturers also produce SDSs in other languages. If you have workers who speak language(s) other than English, you may be able to obtain SDSs in those languages to ensure effective hazard communication.

Employers must maintain copies of SDSs in their workplaces, and must ensure that SDSs are readily accessible to workers when they are in their work areas during their work shifts. This accessibility may be accomplished in many different ways. You must decide what is appropriate for your particular workplace. Some employers keep the SDSs in a binder in a central location (e.g., in a pick-up truck on a construction site). Others, particularly in workplaces with large numbers of chemicals, provide access electronically. However, if access to SDSs is provided electronically, there must be an adequate back-up system in place in the event of a power outage, equipment failure, or other emergency involving the primary electronic system. As long as workers can get the information when they need it, any approach may be used. When workers must travel between workplaces during a work shift, SDSs may be kept at the primary workplace facility. No matter what system

is used, employers must ensure that workers and medical personnel can immediately obtain the required information in an emergency.

In order to ensure that you have a current SDS for each chemical in the plant as required, and that worker access is provided, OSHA's CSHOs will be looking for the following items in your program:

1. Designation of person(s) responsible for obtaining and maintaining the SDSs;

2. How such sheets are maintained in the workplace (e.g., in notebooks in the work area(s) or electronically), and how workers obtain access to them when they are in their work area during the work shift;

3. Procedures to follow when the SDS is not received at the time of the first shipment;

4. An SDS for each hazardous chemical in the workplace, and training of workers that includes review of SDS format and use.

For employers using hazardous chemicals, an important aspect of the hazard communication program is to ensure that someone is responsible for obtaining and maintaining the SDSs for every hazardous chemical in the workplace. To ensure that your hazard communication program improves safety and health with regard to chemical use, you should review the SDSs, and use the information to choose the needed protective measures to prevent or reduce exposures in your workplace. SDSs should be used to evaluate your workplace, and establish a plan to ensure it is safe. The following is a section-by-section description of the information required for each part of the SDS from Appendix D of HazCom 2012. Become familiar with the information available in each section of an SDS so that you will be able to more quickly access this information in an emergency and make better use of the data available.

OSHA has developed a QuickCard™ on SDSs (OSHA 3493) that may be useful in your training program. It is available on the OSHA Hazard Communication web page at www.osha.gov/dsg/hazcom, or from your local OSHA area office.

Minimum Information for an SDS

Heading	Subheading
1. Identification	(a) Product identifier used on the label; (b) Other means of identification; (c) Recommended use of the chemical and restrictions on use; (d) Name, address, and telephone number of the chemical manufacturer, importer, or other responsible party; (e) Emergency phone number.
2. Hazard(s) identification	(a) Classification of the chemical in accordance with paragraph (d) of §1910.1200; (b) Signal word, hazard statement(s), symbol(s) and precautionary statement(s) in accord with paragraph (f) of §1910.1200. (Hazard symbols may be provided as graphical reproductions in black and white or the name of the symbol, e.g., flame, skull and crossbones); (c) Describe any hazards not otherwise classified that have been identified during the classification process; (d) Where an ingredient with unknown acute toxicity is used in a mixture at a concentration ≥ 1% and the mixture is not classified based on testing of the mixture as a whole, a statement that X% of the mixture consists of ingredient(s) of unknown acute toxicity is required.

3. Composition/ information on ingredients	Except as provided for in paragraph (i) of §1910.1200 on trade secrets:
	
	For Substances
	
	(a) Chemical name;
	(b) Common name and synonyms;
	(c) CAS number and other unique identifiers;
	(d) Impurities and stabilizing additives which are themselves classified and which contribute to the classification of the substance.
	
	For Mixtures
	
	In addition to the information required for substances:
	
	(a) The chemical name and concentration (exact percentage) or concentration ranges of all ingredients which are classified as health hazards in accordance with paragraph (d) of §1910.1200 and
	
	    (1) are present above their cut-off/concentration limits; or
	    (2) present a health risk below the cut-off/concentration limits.
	
	(b) The concentration (exact percentage) shall be specified unless a trade secret claim is made in accordance with paragraph (i) of §1910.1200, when there is batch-to-batch variability in the production of a mixture, or for a group of substantially similar mixtures (*See* A.0.5.1.2) with similar chemical composition. In these cases, concentration ranges may be used.
	
	For All Chemicals Where a Trade Secret is Claimed
	
	Where a trade secret is claimed in accordance with paragraph (i) of §1910.1200, a statement that the specific chemical identity and/or exact percentage (concentration) of composition has been withheld as a trade secret is required.

Heading	Subheading
4. First-aid measures	(a) Description of necessary measures, subdivided according to the different routes of exposure, i.e., inhalation, skin and eye contact, and ingestion; (b) Most important symptoms/effects, acute and delayed; (c) Indication of immediate medical attention and special treatment needed, if necessary.
5. Firefighting measures	(a) Suitable (and unsuitable) extinguishing media; (b) Specific hazards arising from the chemical (e.g., nature of any hazardous combustion products); (c) Special protective equipment and precautions for firefighters.
6. Accidental release measures	(a) Personal precautions, protective equipment, and emergency procedures; (b) Methods and materials for containment and cleaning up.
7. Handling and storage	(a) Precautions for safe handling; (b) Conditions for safe storage, including any incompatibilities.
8. Exposure controls/ personal protection	(a) OSHA permissible exposure limit (PEL), American Conference of Governmental Industrial Hygienists (ACGIH) Threshold Limit Value (TLV), and any other exposure limit used or recommended by the chemical manufacturer, importer, or employer preparing the safety data sheet, where available; (b) Appropriate engineering controls; (c) Individual protection measures, such as personal protective equipment.
9. Physical and chemical properties	(a) Appearance (physical state, color, etc.); (b) Odor; (c) Odor threshold; (d) pH; (e) Melting point/freezing point; (f) Initial boiling point and boiling range; (g) Flash point; (h) Evaporation rate; (i) Flammability (solid, gas); (j) Upper/lower flammability or explosive limits; (k) Vapor pressure; (l) Vapor density; (m) Relative density; (n) Solubility(ies); (o) Partition coefficient: n-octanol/water; (p) Auto-ignition temperature; (q) Decomposition temperature; (r) Viscosity.

Heading	Subheading
10. Stability and reactivity	(a) Reactivity; (b) Chemical stability; (c) Possibility of hazardous reactions; (d) Conditions to avoid (e.g., static discharge, shock, or vibration); (e) Incompatible materials; (f) Hazardous decomposition products.
11. Toxicological information	Description of the various toxicological (health) effects and the available data used to identify those effects, including: (a) Information on the likely routes of exposure (inhalation, ingestion, skin and eye contact); (b) Symptoms related to the physical, chemical and toxicological characteristics; (c) Delayed and immediate effects and also chronic effects from short- and long-term exposure; (d) Numerical measures of toxicity (such as acute toxicity estimates); (e) Whether the hazardous chemical is listed in the National Toxicology Program (NTP) Report on Carcinogens (latest edition) or has been found to be a potential carcinogen in the International Agency for Research on Cancer (IARC) Monographs (latest edition), or by OSHA.
12. Ecological information (Non-mandatory)	(a) Ecotoxicity (aquatic and terrestrial, where available); (b) Persistence and degradability; (c) Bioaccumulative potential; (d) Mobility in soil; (e) Other adverse effects (such as hazardous to the ozone layer).
13. Disposal considerations (Non-mandatory)	Description of waste residues and information on their safe handling and methods of disposal, including the disposal of any contaminated packaging.
14. Transport information (Non-mandatory)	(a) UN number; (b) UN proper shipping name; (c) Transport hazard class(es); (d) Packing group, if applicable; (e) Environmental hazards (e.g., Marine pollutant (Yes/No)); (f) Transport in bulk (according to Annex II of MARPOL 73/78 and the IBC Code); (g) Special precautions which a user needs to be aware of, or needs to comply with, in connection with transport or conveyance either within or outside their premises.
15. Regulatory information (Non-mandatory)	Safety, health and environmental regulations specific for the product in question.
16. Other information, including date of preparation or last revision	The date of preparation of the SDS or the last change to it.

5. Inform and Train Employees

- Train employees on the hazardous chemicals in their work area before initial assignment, and when new hazards are introduced.
- Include the requirements of the standard, hazards of chemicals, appropriate protective measures, and where and how to obtain additional information.

The third part of the hazard communication approach in HazCom 2012 is employee information and training **(paragraph (h) Employee Information and Training)**. The key requirement is in paragraph (h)(1):

(h)(1) Employers shall provide employees with effective information and training on hazardous chemicals in their work area at the time of their initial assignment, and whenever a new chemical hazard the employees have not previously been trained about is introduced into their work area. Information and training may be designed to cover categories of hazards (e.g., flammability, carcinogenicity) or specific chemicals. Chemical-specific information must always be available through labels and safety data sheets.

For information and training to be effective, the workers in the training must comprehend the hazards in the workplace and ways to protect themselves. OSHA does not expect that workers will be able to recall and recite all data provided about each hazardous chemical in the workplace. What is most important is that workers understand that they are exposed to hazardous chemicals, know how to read labels and SDSs, and have a general understanding of what information is provided in these documents, and how to access these tools. Workers must also be aware of the protective measures available in their workplace, how to use or implement these measures, and who they should contact if an issue arises.

Information and training may be done either by individual chemical, or by hazard classes and categories (such as acute toxicity or flammable liquids). If there are only a few chemicals in the workplace, then you may want to discuss each one individually. Where there are large numbers of

chemicals, or the chemicals change frequently, you will probably want to train generally based on the hazard classes and categories. Workers must have access to the substance-specific information on the labels and SDSs.

HazCom 2012 requires employers to both provide certain information to employees and to train employees. The standard requires employees to be informed of:

- The general requirements of the Hazard Communication Standard;
- Where hazardous chemicals are located in their work areas (operations where exposure may occur); and,
- What the workplace hazard communication program includes, and where and how they can access the program.

Training, on the other hand, is a more active process. The training conducted to comply with HazCom 2012 must address the following:

- Methods and observations that may be used to detect the presence or release of a hazardous chemical in the work area (such as monitoring conducted by the employer, continuous monitoring devices, visual appearance or odor of hazardous chemicals when being released, etc.);
- The physical, health, simple asphyxiation, combustible dust and pyrophoric gas hazards, as well as hazards not otherwise classified, of the chemicals in the work area;
- The measures employees can take to protect themselves from these hazards, including specific procedures the employer has implemented to protect employees from

exposure to hazardous chemicals, such as appropriate work practices, emergency procedures, and personal protective equipment to be used; and,

■ The details of the hazard communication program developed by the employer, including an explanation of the labels received on shipped containers and the workplace labeling system used by their employer; the SDS, including the format of the SDS (where each type of information is located) and how employees can obtain and use the appropriate hazard information.

A properly conducted training program will ensure worker comprehension and understanding. It is not sufficient to either just read material to the workers, or simply hand them material to read. As explained in Dr. Michaels' *OSHA Training Standards Policy Statement* (April 28, 2010), OSHA requires employers to present information in a manner and language that their employees can understand. If employers customarily need to communicate work instructions or other workplace information to employees in a language other than English, they will also need to provide safety and health training to employees in the same manner. Similarly, if the employee's vocabulary is limited, the training must account for that limitation. By the same token, if employees are not literate, telling them to read training materials will not satisfy the employer's training obligation.

In conducting a training program, you want to create a climate where workers feel free to ask questions. This will help you to ensure that the information is understood. You must always remember that the underlying purpose of the HCS is to reduce the incidence of chemical source illnesses and injuries. This will be accomplished by modifying behavior through the provision of hazard information and information about protective measures. If your program works, you and your workers will better understand the chemical hazards in the workplace, and how to protect workers from experiencing adverse effects. The procedures you establish regarding, for example, purchasing, storing, and handling of these chemicals will improve, and thereby reduce the risks posed to workers exposed to the chemical hazards involved.

Furthermore, your workers' comprehension will also be increased, and proper work practices will be more likely followed in your workplace.

If you are going to do the training yourself, you will have to understand the material and be prepared to motivate the workers to learn. This is not always an easy task, but the benefits are worth the effort. More information regarding appropriate training can be found in Appendix B of this guide, which provides steps to follow in setting up and conducting training.

In reviewing your hazard communication program with regard to information and training, the following items need to be considered:

1. Designation of person(s) responsible for conducting training;

2. Format of the program to be used (audiovisuals, classroom instruction, etc.);

3. Elements of the information and training program (should be consistent with the elements in paragraph (h) of the standard); and,

4. Procedure to train new workers at the time of their initial assignment to work with a hazardous chemical, and to train workers when a new chemical hazard is introduced into the workplace.

The written program should provide enough details about the employer's plans in this area to assess whether or not a good faith effort is being made to train workers. When assessing an employer's compliance with hazard communication training requirements, OSHA CSHOs will talk to workers to determine if they have received training, if they know they are exposed to hazardous chemicals, and if they know where to obtain substance-specific information on labels and SDSs. It should be noted that if workers do not speak English, the employer must convey the hazard communication information in the language they understand—just like other job requirements and instructions are provided. OSHA has bilingual CSHOs, and they will be speaking to workers who speak another language to determine compliance.

The standard does not require employers to maintain records of employee training, but many employers choose to do so. This may help you monitor your own program to ensure that all workers are appropriately trained. Keeping records that document who was trained, when the training was conducted, and what was covered is also helpful to document compliance with OSHA's training requirement in case of an inspection. The standard does not require retraining on a regular schedule, it simply requires retraining if there is a new chemical hazard introduced into the work area. If your initial training program includes all potential hazards covered by HazCom 2012, there is no retraining required. However, it is good business practice to repeat and reinforce what is learned in training to make sure that workers retain the hazard information.

If you already have a hazard communication training program, you may simply have to update it to comply with HazCom 2012. In particular, by December 1, 2013, you will need to train your employees about the new label and SDS formats they will be seeing in their work areas. Additional hazard training is not required if you have already trained under the existing hazard communication requirements. However, after you receive all of the new labels and SDSs, and have updated your hazard communication program, you may find that

there is a type of hazard on which employees have not yet received training. You will need to train employees on these new hazards at the time you become aware of the new hazard. If you become aware of new hazards after December 1, 2015, you will have until June 1, 2016 to ensure those hazards are included in the hazard communication program, the workplace labeling reflects these new hazards, and employees are trained on these new hazards.

An employer can provide employees information and training through whatever means are found appropriate. Although there will always have to be some training onsite (such as informing workers of the location and availability of the written program and SDSs), employee training may be satisfied in part by general training about the requirements of the HCS and about chemical hazards on the job which is provided by, for example, trade associations, unions, colleges, and professional schools. In addition, previous training, education and experience of a worker may relieve the employer of some of the burdens of informing and training that worker. Regardless of the method relied upon, however, the employer is always ultimately responsible for ensuring that workers are adequately trained. If the CSHO finds that the training is deficient, the employer will be cited for the deficiency regardless of who actually provided the training on behalf of the employer.

6. Evaluate and Reassess Your Program

- Review your hazard communication program periodically to make sure that it is still working and meeting its objectives.
- Revise your program as appropriate to address changed conditions in the workplace (e.g., new chemicals, new hazards, etc.).

Because your hazard communication program must remain up to date, it will be necessary to periodically evaluate and reassess your program.

The information in your written program must be accurate. The list of hazardous chemicals required to be maintained as part of the written program will serve as an inventory. As new chemicals are purchased, the list must be updated. Revisions to the inventory of chemicals should be made when you eliminate chemicals in the workplace, or when you bring in a new chemical. The inventory also can be used to ensure that you have SDSs for all chemicals in the workplace, and such revisions are key to ensuring that is achieved. In addition, designation of people to handle different parts of the program should also be current and accurate. Many companies have found it convenient to include on their purchase orders the name and address of the person designated in their company to receive SDSs to help maintain a complete set.

Program coordinators should routinely walk around the workplace to check that containers are labeled as required and that workers are following established work practices to protect themselves from chemical exposure. Proactive monitoring of the workplace is critical to ensuring compliance with the HCS.

As new SDSs are received, there should be a process in place to review them and determine whether any handling procedures need to change to protect against the hazards of these chemicals. Using information on the SDS effectively will make safer workplace conditions a standard business practice in your facility.

This simple checklist will help to ensure that you are in compliance with the standard:

Obtained/accessed a copy of the standard. ____
Read and understood the requirements. ____
Assigned responsibility for tasks. ____
Prepared an inventory of chemicals. ____
Ensured that containers are labeled. ____
Obtained SDSs for each chemical. ____
Prepared written program. ____
Made SDSs available to workers. ____
Conducted training for workers. ____
Established procedures to maintain current program. ____
Established procedures to evaluate program effectiveness, including maintenance of SDSs. ____

III. CONCLUSION

OSHA believes that the Hazard Communication Standard is of critical importance to ensuring that hazardous chemicals are identified, and that proper measures are implemented in workplaces to achieve safe use and handling. By understanding the hazards of the chemicals, and using available information to pick the proper control measures to address these hazards, employers can achieve many benefits for themselves, as well as for their exposed workers. HazCom 2012 provides the framework for building a chemical safety and health management program in a workplace. Figure 6 illustrates the steps that have been discussed to ensure that a workplace hazard communication program is effective.

Figure 6: An Effective Hazard Communication Program

APPENDIX A: SAMPLE WRITTEN HAZARD COMMUNICATION PROGRAM

The following sample hazard communication program is based on the requirements of the Hazard Communication Standard (HazCom 2012), 29 CFR 1910.1200. The intent of this sample is to provide an easy-to-use format that can be modified to address the specific situation in your workplace. You are free to use whatever format you choose to develop your program—there is no requirement to follow this example. However, if you use this or any other sample program, you must customize it to your specific workplace, otherwise you will not be in compliance with the HCS.

HAZARD COMMUNICATION PROGRAM

1. Company Policy

To ensure that information about the dangers of all hazardous chemicals used by (*Name of Company*) is known by all affected workers, the following hazard communication program has been implemented. Under this program, workers will be informed of the requirements of the OSHA Hazard Communication Standard, the operations where exposure to hazardous chemicals may occur, and how workers can access this program, as well as labels and SDSs.

This program applies to any chemical which is known to be present in the workplace in such a manner that workers may be exposed under normal conditions of use or in a foreseeable emergency. All work areas that involve potential exposure to chemicals are part of the hazard communication program. Copies of the hazard communication program are available in the (**location**) for review by any interested worker.

(*Name of responsible person and/or position*) is the program coordinator, with overall responsibility for the program, including reviewing and updating this plan as necessary.

2. Container Labeling

(*Name of responsible person and/or position*) will verify that all containers received for use will be clearly labeled in accord with the requirements of HazCom 2012, including a product identifier, pictogram, hazard statement, signal word, and precautionary statements, as well as the supplier's contact information (name and address).

The (*name of responsible person and/or position*) in each work area will ensure that all secondary containers are labeled with the original supplier's label or with an alternative workplace label. For help with labeling, see (*name of responsible person and/or position*).

On the following individual stationary process containers, we are using (*description of labeling system used*) rather than a label to convey the required information:

(*List containers here*)

We are using an in-house labeling system (*describe any in-house system which conveys required workplace label information*).

The (*name of responsible person and/or position*) will review the company labeling procedures every (*provide a time period*) and will update labels as required.

3. Safety Data Sheets (SDSs)

The (*name of responsible person and/or position*) is responsible for establishing and monitoring the company SDS program. The procedure below will be followed when an SDS is not received at the time of initial shipment:

(*Describe procedure to be followed here*)

Copies of SDSs for all hazardous chemicals to which workers are exposed or are potentially exposed will be kept in (*identify location*). Workers can access SDSs by (*insert procedure for access*).

Note: If alternatives to paper copies of SDSs are used, describe the format used and how workers can access the SDSs.

SDSs will be readily available to all workers in each work area during each work shift. If an SDS is not available, contact (*name of responsible person and/or position*).

When revised SDSs are received, the following procedures will be followed to replace old SDSs:

(*Describe procedures*)

The (*name of responsible person and/or position*) is responsible for reviewing the SDSs received for safety and health implications, and initiating any needed changes in workplace practices.

4. Employee Information and Training

(*Name of responsible person and/or position*) is responsible for employee information and training.

Every worker who will be potentially exposed to hazardous chemicals will receive initial training on the Hazard Communication standard and this program before starting work.

The training program for new workers is as follows (*describe how the training will be presented, and what it will include*).

Prior to introducing a new chemical hazard into any work area, each worker in that work area will be given information and training as outlined above for the new chemical hazard. The training format will be as follows:

(*Describe training format, such as audiovisuals, interactive computer programs, classroom instruction, etc.*)

5. Hazards of Non-routine Tasks

Periodically, workers are required to perform non-routine tasks that are hazardous. Examples of non-routine tasks are: confined space entry, tank cleaning, and painting reactor vessels. Prior to starting work on such projects, each affected worker will be given information by (*Name of responsible person and/or position*) about the hazardous chemicals he or she may encounter during such activity. This information will include specific chemical hazards, protective and safety measures the worker should use, and steps the company is taking to reduce the hazards, including ventilation, respirators, the presence of another worker (buddy systems), and emergency procedures.

6. Informing Other Employers/Contractors

It is the responsibility of (*Name of responsible person and/or position*) to provide other employers and contractors with information about hazardous chemicals that their workers may be exposed to on this work site, and suggested precautions for workers. It is the responsibility of (*Name of responsible person and/or position*) to obtain information about hazardous chemicals used by other employers to which our workers may be exposed.

Other employers and contractors will be provided with SDSs for hazardous chemicals generated by this company's operations in the following manner:

(*Describe company policy here*)

In addition to providing a copy of an SDS to other employers, other employers will be informed of necessary precautionary measures to protect workers exposed to operations performed by this company.

Also, other employers will be informed of the hazard labels used by the company. If alternative workplace labeling systems are used, the other employers will be provided with information to understand the labels used for hazardous chemicals to which their workers may have exposure.

7. List of Hazardous Chemicals

A list of all known hazardous chemicals in the workplace is attached to this program. This list includes the name of each chemical, and the work area(s) in which each of the chemicals is used. Further information on each chemical may be obtained from the SDSs, located in (**identify location**).

When new chemicals are received, this list is updated within (x) days of introduction into the workplace. To ensure that any new chemical is added in a timely manner, the following procedures shall be followed:

(Identify procedures to be followed)

The hazardous chemical inventory is compiled and maintained by (**Name of responsible person and/ or position and telephone number**).

8. Chemicals in Unlabeled Pipes

Work activities may be performed by workers in areas where chemicals are transferred through unlabeled pipes. Prior to starting work in these areas, the worker shall be informed by *(Name of responsible person and/or position)* about the identity and hazards of the chemicals in the pipe, as well as required precautionary measures required to be followed.

9. Program Availability

A copy of this program will be made available, upon request, to workers, their designated representatives, and OSHA.

APPENDIX B:
QUICK GUIDE TO HAZARD COMMUNICATION TRAINING

The Hazard Communication Standard (HCS) (29 CFR 1910.1200) requires employers that have hazardous chemicals in their workplaces to implement a hazard communication program. The program includes information about labels on containers, safety data sheets (SDSs), and training for workers. Each employer must describe in a written program how it will meet the requirements of the HCS in each of these areas.

For employers that use chemicals, rather than produce them, labels and SDSs are received with the products they purchase. These written documents form the basis of the hazard communication program, providing information for both employers and workers about the hazards of the chemicals, as well as ways to protect people from experiencing adverse effects as a result of their use. Training is the last step to be undertaken to implement an effective hazard communication program. Through proper training, the employer has the opportunity to ensure that workers understand the hazards of the chemicals they work with, as well as what steps to take to ensure that they are protected from them. It also introduces them to labels and SDSs, explaining how to access these documents in their own workplace to obtain additional information. Training is therefore a critical part of the approach to hazard communication, tying together the three major components in an understandable form.

Before providing training, the employer should have a basic understanding of the requirements of the HCS, and have prepared its hazard communication program. This quick guide will focus on what is needed to set up a hazard communication training program. It is based on *Training Requirements in OSHA Standards and Training Guidelines* (OSHA 2254) developed by OSHA to assist employers to design any type of occupational safety and health training program, but relates the Guidelines specifically to hazard communication. It is a step-by-step approach. OSHA has also developed a series of QuickCards™ on elements of the training that employers may find useful: www.osha.gov/dsg/hazcom/ghsquickcards.html.

Training Step	Factors to Consider
Determining if training is needed	Are workers potentially exposed to hazardous chemicals in your workplace? You can determine this by reviewing the labels received on containers of chemicals you use, as well as safety data sheets (SDSs). You must have a hazard communication program if you have workers who are potentially exposed to hazardous chemicals. Training workers is part of the required hazard communication program. Therefore, training is needed wherever workers are potentially exposed to hazardous chemicals in their workplaces.
Identifying training needs	Workers must be trained before they are initially assigned to work where they are potentially exposed to a hazardous chemical. Therefore, if you have never provided training before, you must train all workers who are potentially exposed. Once this initial training is completed, you must train any new workers who are hired and will be working with hazardous chemicals. You must also provide training whenever a new hazard is introduced, or when workers change jobs and therefore face potential exposures. While training is not required to be repeated on a regular basis, you may want to consider doing that to be sure that workers remember what they have learned. It is also a good opportunity for you to review your hazard communication program, and make sure that it is still working effectively.

Training Step	Factors to Consider
Identifying goals and objectives	Compliance with the requirements of the Hazard Communication Standard is a primary goal. Compliance will promote a safer workplace by ensuring that the potential hazards of chemicals are known both to you and to your workers. In addition, the measures to follow to prevent adverse health or physical effects resulting from chemical exposures should be familiar to everyone in the workplace. Preparing for the training gives you an opportunity to review the hazards of the chemicals you have in the workplace, and to consider substituting less hazardous chemicals where appropriate. It also allows you to review the protective measures you have in place to ensure that they are working, and to consider other types of protection as well. Implementation of a hazard communication program should be useful both to employers that have hazardous chemicals as part of their workplace processes, and to workers who are exposed to those chemicals. Training ties together all of the aspects of the workplace hazard communication program to relate it to the actual workplace conditions. Thus both employers and workers should be more familiar with the hazards present, know what steps must be taken to control those hazards, and be assured that the workplace is safer. They should also know how to obtain more information when needed from the container labels and the SDSs.

You may want to consider if you have any additional learning objectives you would like to accomplish through this training program. For example, you may also have compliance obligations for related standards that could be combined into this program and accomplished in one training session (such as training required under the Respiratory Protection standard). Also, it may be an opportunity to review safe work practices and ways to perform jobs in a more efficient manner, and tie this into avoiding chemical hazards. |
| **Identifying learning activities** | The Hazard Communication Standard specifies what information must be provided to workers:

• The requirements of the Hazard Communication Standard;
• Any operations in their work area where hazardous chemicals are present; and
• The location and availability of the written hazard communication program, including the required list(s) of hazardous chemicals, and SDSs required by the standard.

In addition to providing this information to workers, they must be trained on the following:

• Methods and observations that may be used to detect the presence or release of a hazardous chemical in the work area (such as monitoring conducted by the employer, continuous monitoring devices, visual appearance or odor of hazardous chemicals when being released, etc.);
• The physical and health hazards of the chemicals in the work area;
• The measures workers can take to protect themselves from these hazards, including specific procedures the employer has implemented to protect workers from exposure to hazardous chemicals, such as appropriate work practices, emergency procedures, and personal protective equipment to be used; and
• The details of the hazard communication program developed by the employer, including an explanation of the labeling system and the SDS, and how workers can obtain and use the appropriate information.

The way in which this information is conveyed is left up to the trainer to determine. You can use any type of media available to you (such as slides, videos, computer interactive programs). Combinations of media are often an effective way to keep the workers' attention. In addition, active participation is important, so you may want to include learning activities that allow the workers to participate and have hands-on experiences. Relating the information to their specific workplace conditions helps to ensure that you meet the requirements of the standard, as well as improving learning and making the training more interesting. |

Training Step	Factors to Consider
Conducting the training	**Preparation:** In order to train workers under the Hazard Communication Standard, the trainer must be familiar with: • the requirements of the standard that apply to the workplace; • the hazardous chemicals in the workplace to which workers are potentially exposed, as well as the types of hazards they pose; • the hazard communication program implemented in the workplace; and • the protective measures being employed in the workplace to prevent adverse effects from occurring. In addition to being thoroughly familiar with the material to be covered in the training, the trainer must be aware of the facilities available for the training, including the physical location, the type of equipment (e.g., a PowerPoint projector, computer), and plan the training session accordingly based on the conditions. **Presenting the training:** The purpose of the training is to convey information that is important to the student, and will achieve a safer workplace. Care should be taken to ensure that the facilities are conducive to a successful training session, and that the presentation is done in a way that motivates learning and a positive outcome. Worker participation helps to ensure that the learning objectives are accomplished. This can be done through hands-on examples, discussions, and other active means of conveying the required information.
Evaluating program effectiveness	Consideration should be given to including some sort of evaluation tool in the training to obtain feedback from the workers on the presentation, what formats might work better, and what they learned. This could be in the form of a sheet to be filled out by workers after the training. In evaluating the effectiveness of the program, you should observe how the training has changed worker behavior. For example, if workers have better compliance with use of protective measures (such as wearing gloves when appropriate), this could factor into the evaluation of the program.
Improving the training	The trainers should use their own impressions as well as feedback from the students to improve the training before it is presented again. If workers are not interested in the training as it is conducted, do not appear motivated, and do not exhibit an increased knowledge of hazards and the use of protective practices, it may be necessary to review and revise the training to achieve a better outcome.

Following these seven steps should enable you to design and implement an effective hazard communication training program. A safer workplace benefits the employer as well as the worker, and their shared interest in this goal should help to achieve effective hazard communication training.

WORKERS' RIGHTS

Under OSHA law, workers are entitled to working conditions that do not pose a risk of serious harm. To help assure a safe and healthful workplace, the law provides workers with the right to:

- File a confidential complaint with OSHA to have their workplace inspected.

- Receive information and training about hazards, methods to prevent harm, and the OSHA standards that apply to their workplace. The training must be done in a language and vocabulary workers can understand.

- Receive copies of records of work-related injuries and illnesses that occur in their workplace.

- Receive copies of the results from tests and monitoring done to find and measure hazards in their workplace.

- Receive copies of their workplace medical records.

- Participate in an OSHA inspection and speak in private with the inspector.

- File a complaint with OSHA if they have been retaliated against by their employer as the result of requesting an inspection or using any of their other rights under the OSH Act.

- File a complaint if punished or retaliated against for acting as a "whistleblower" under the 21 additional federal laws for which OSHA has jurisdiction.

For more information, visit OSHA's Workers' Rights page at www.osha.gov/workers.html.

OSHA ASSISTANCE, SERVICES AND PROGRAMS

OSHA offers free compliance assistance to employers and workers. Several OSHA programs and services can help employers identify and correct job hazards, as well as improve their injury and illness prevention program.

Establishing an Injury and Illness Prevention Program

The key to a safe and healthful work environment is a comprehensive injury and illness prevention program.

Injury and illness prevention programs are systems that can substantially reduce the number and severity of workplace injuries and illnesses, while reducing costs to employers. Thousands of employers across the United States already manage safety using illness and injury prevention programs, and OSHA believes that all employers can and should do the same. Thirty-four states have requirements or voluntary guidelines for workplace injury and illness prevention programs.

Most successful injury and illness prevention programs are based on a common set of key elements. These include management leadership, worker participation, hazard identification, hazard prevention and control, education and training, and program evaluation and improvement. Visit OSHA's illness and injury prevention program web page at www.osha.gov/dsg/topics/safetyhealth for more information.

Compliance Assistance Specialists

OSHA has compliance assistance specialists throughout the nation located in most OSHA offices. Compliance assistance specialists can provide information to employers and workers about OSHA standards, short educational programs on specific hazards or OSHA rights and responsibilities, and information on additional compliance assistance resources. For more details, visit www.osha.gov/dcsp/compliance_assistance/cas.html or call 1-800-321-OSHA [6742] to contact your local OSHA office.

Free On-site Safety and Health Consultation Services for Small Business

OSHA's On-site Consultation Program offers free and confidential advice to small and medium-sized businesses in all states across the country, with priority given to high-hazard worksites. Each year, responding to requests from small employers looking to create or improve their safety and health management programs, OSHA's On-site Consultation Program conducts over 29,000 visits to small business worksites covering over 1.5 million workers across the nation.

On-site consultation services are separate from enforcement and do not result in penalties or citations. Consultants from state agencies or universities work with employers to identify workplace hazards, provide advice on compliance with OSHA standards, and assist in establishing safety and health management programs.

For more information, to find the local On-site Consultation office in your state, or to request a brochure on Consultation Services, visit www.osha.gov/consultation, or call 1-800-321-OSHA [6742].

Under the consultation program, certain exemplary employers may request participation in OSHA's **Safety and Health Achievement Recognition Program (SHARP)**. Eligibility for participation includes, but is not limited to, receiving a full-service, comprehensive consultation visit, correcting all identified hazards and developing an effective safety and health management program. Worksites that receive SHARP recognition are exempt from programmed inspections during the period that the SHARP certification is valid.

Cooperative Programs

OSHA offers cooperative programs under which businesses, labor groups and other organizations can work cooperatively with OSHA. To find out more about any of the following programs, visit www.osha.gov/dcsp/compliance_assistance/index_programs.html.

Strategic Partnerships and Alliances

The OSHA Strategic Partnerships (OSP) provides the opportunity for OSHA to partner with employers, workers, professional or trade associations, labor organizations, and/or other interested stakeholders. OSHA Strategic Partnerships are formalized through unique agreements designed to encourage, assist, and recognize partner efforts to eliminate serious hazards and achieve model workplace safety and health practices. Through the Alliance Program, OSHA works with groups committed to worker safety and health to prevent workplace fatalities, injuries and illnesses by developing compliance assistance tools and resources to share with workers and employers, and educate workers and employers about their rights and responsibilities.

Voluntary Protection Programs (VPP)

The VPP recognize employers and workers in private industry and federal agencies who have implemented effective safety and health management programs and maintain injury and illness rates below the national average for their respective industries. In VPP, management, labor, and OSHA work cooperatively and proactively to prevent fatalities, injuries, and illnesses through a system focused on: hazard prevention and control, worksite analysis, training, and management commitment and worker involvement.

Occupational Safety and Health Training

The OSHA Training Institute in Arlington Heights, Illinois, provides basic and advanced training and education in safety and health for federal and state compliance officers, state consultants, other federal agency personnel and private sector employers, workers, and their representatives. In addition, 27 OSHA Training Institute Education Centers at 42 locations throughout the United States deliver courses on OSHA standards and occupational safety and health issues to thousands of students a year.

For more information on training, contact the OSHA Directorate of Training and Education, 2020 Arlington Heights Road, Arlington Heights, IL 60005; call 1-847-297-4810; or visit www.osha.gov.

OSHA Educational Materials

OSHA has many types of educational materials in English, Spanish, Vietnamese and other languages available in print or online. These include:

- Brochures/booklets that cover a wide variety of job hazards and other topics;

- Fact Sheets, which contain basic background information on safety and health hazards;

- Guidance documents that provide detailed examinations of specific safety and health issues;

- Online Safety and Health Topics pages;

- Posters;

- Small, laminated QuickCards™ that provide brief safety and health information; and

- *QuickTakes*, OSHA's free, twice-monthly online newsletter with the latest news about OSHA initiatives and products to assist employers and workers in finding and preventing workplace hazards. To sign up for *QuickTakes* visit OSHA's web site at www.osha.gov and click on *QuickTakes* at the top of the page.

To view materials available online or for a listing of free publications, visit OSHA's web site at www. osha.gov. You can also call 1-800-321-OSHA [6742] to order publications.

OSHA's web site also has a variety of eTools. These include utilities such as expert advisors, electronic compliance assistance, videos and other information for employers and workers. To learn more about OSHA's safety and health tools online, visit www.osha.gov.

NIOSH HEALTH HAZARD EVALUATION PROGRAM

Getting Help with Health Hazards

The National Institute for Occupational Safety and Health (NIOSH) is a federal agency that conducts scientific and medical research on workers' safety and health. At no cost to employers or workers, NIOSH can help identify health hazards and recommend ways to reduce or eliminate those hazards in the workplace through its Health Hazard Evaluation (HHE) Program.

Workers, union representatives and employers can request a NIOSH HHE. An HHE is often requested when there is a higher than expected rate of a disease or injury in a group of workers. These situations may be the result of an unknown cause, a new hazard, or a mixture of sources. To request a NIOSH Health Hazard Evaluation go to www. cdc.gov/niosh/hhe/request.html. To find out more about the Health Hazard Evaluation Program:

- Call (513) 841-4382, or to talk to a staff member in Spanish, call (513) 841-4439; or

- Send an email to HHERequestHelp@cdc.gov.

OSHA REGIONAL OFFICES

Region I
Boston Regional Office
(CT*, ME, MA, NH, RI, VT*)
JFK Federal Building, Room E340
Boston, MA 02203
(617) 565-9860 (617) 565-9827 Fax

Region II
New York Regional Office
(NJ*, NY*, PR*, VI*)
201 Varick Street, Room 670
New York, NY 10014
(212) 337-2378 (212) 337-2371 Fax

Region III
Philadelphia Regional Office
(DE, DC, MD*, PA, VA*, WV)
The Curtis Center
170 S. Independence Mall West
Suite 740 West
Philadelphia, PA 19106-3309
(215) 861-4900 (215) 861-4904 Fax

Region IV
Atlanta Regional Office
(AL, FL, GA, KY*, MS, NC*, SC*, TN*)
61 Forsyth Street, SW, Room 6T50
Atlanta, GA 30303
(678) 237-0400 (678) 237-0447 Fax

Region V
Chicago Regional Office
(IL*, IN*, MI*, MN*, OH, WI)
230 South Dearborn Street
Room 3244
Chicago, IL 60604
(312) 353-2220 (312) 353-7774 Fax

Region VI
Dallas Regional Office
(AR, LA, NM*, OK, TX)
525 Griffin Street, Room 602
Dallas, TX 75202
(972) 850-4145 (972) 850-4149 Fax
(972) 850-4150 FSO Fax

Region VII
Kansas City Regional Office
(IA*, KS, MO, NE)
Two Pershing Square Building
2300 Main Street, Suite 1010
Kansas City, MO 64108-2416
(816) 283-8745 (816) 283-0547 Fax

Region VIII
Denver Regional Office
(CO, MT, ND, SD, UT*, WY*)
Cesar Chavez Memorial Building
1244 Speer Boulevard, Suite 551
Denver, CO 80204
(720) 264-6550 (720) 264-6585 Fax

Region IX
San Francisco Regional Office
(AZ*, CA*, HI*, NV*, and American Samoa,
Guam and the Northern Mariana Islands)
90 7th Street, Suite 18100
San Francisco, CA 94103
(415) 625-2547 (415) 625-2534 Fax

Region X
Seattle Regional Office
(AK*, ID, OR*, WA*)
300 Fifth Avenue, Suite 1280
Seattle, WA 98104
(206) 757-6700 (206) 757-6705 Fax

* These states and territories operate their own
OSHA-approved job safety and health plans and
cover state and local government employees as
well as private sector employees. The Connecticut,
Illinois, New Jersey, New York and Virgin Islands
programs cover public employees only. (Private
sector workers in these states are covered by
Federal OSHA). States with approved programs
must have standards that are identical to, or at
least as effective as, the Federal OSHA standards.

Note: To get contact information for OSHA area
offices, OSHA-approved state plans and OSHA
consultation projects, please visit us online at
www.osha.gov or call us at 1-800-321-OSHA (6742).

HOW TO CONTACT OSHA

For questions or to get information or advice, to report an emergency, report a fatality or catastrophe, order publications, sign up for OSHA's e-newsletter *QuickTakes*, or to file a confidential complaint, contact your nearest OSHA office, visit www.osha.gov or call OSHA at 1-800-321-OSHA (6742), TTY 1-877-889-5627.

For assistance, contact us.
We are OSHA. We can help.

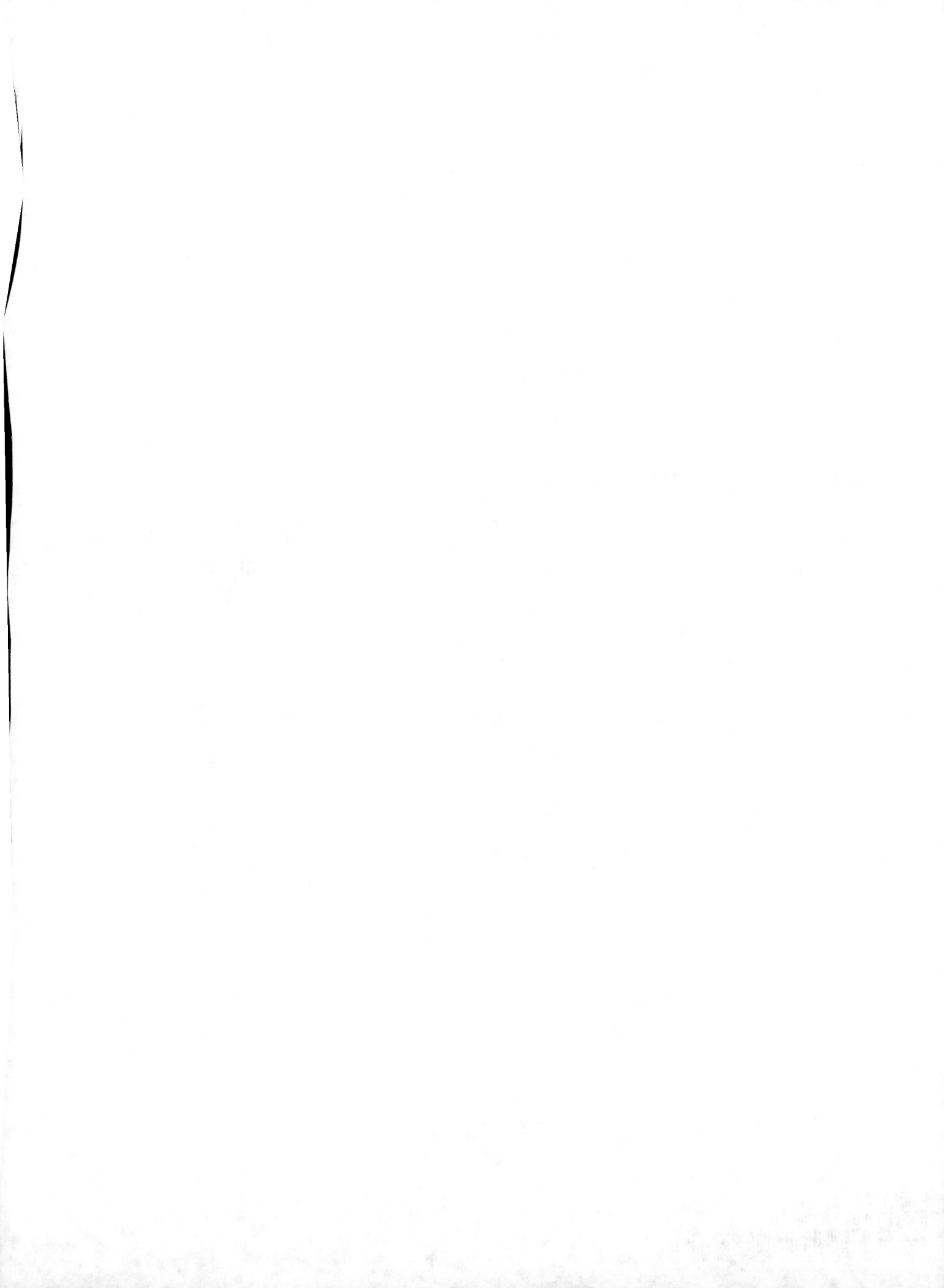